Normal Behavior

Kat Thanopoulos

Presentation by *BookLeaf Publishing*

Web: www.bookleafpub.com

E-mail: info@bookleafpub.com

ISBN: 9789360940942

First edition 2024

To SPM

ACKNOWLEDGEMENT

Thank you to all the people and places that inspire me: my comedy folks, my Greek friends, my original writing partner Bella, a certain unknown Breakers Palm Beach employee, Chicago, Isla and Angela, my Nice Guy Cool Guys, and anyone who cares to read a single word I write. Special thank you to Hellenic International Studies in the Arts and everyone there for bringing me back to writing in a new way. Love you always MB.

A Real Life

And I'm hiding and pretending.
I watch and wonder.
Let my mind convince itself that the memories it holds resemble
that of a life.
I think I will never get that life back.
Real life.
Right?

Love For

I've got a love for logic
But I'm swayed by you

And everything's sweeter because
We're the same height

Babies making potions in the bathtub
I know, you're actually an inch taller

Sing me your folk song and I'll sing you mine
Your face in the cracks of the leather

My little ghost for now
Until I see you again

My Favorite Song

It's a song I like to have
To fill my ears
It demands and grates
Softens and thrums

My favorite song –
Though made in a minute
Has more heart
Than any I've heard yet

I sing the chorus every day
And the words, they change
Notes I've come to love
Fallen off and far away

The missing parts I search for
I hate this metaphor
But I can't separate
From the beat, the tune

Caught in my head so
Other songs I play
To drown it out
But when silence comes

I'm met with you

Cultivation and Reward

What's worth it
What's a quarter
A dime
Spend time
Picking weeds
Growing limes
Cutting grass
Just right
I'll get fruit
And get you too
And get a bruise

The deer got over the fence
That's okay
We all need to eat somehow
Sustenance and maintenance

Fill your throat
With everything I can't,
Dear deer

Normal Behavior

Do they notice when we're not talking?
The friends on the bench,
The workout class,
Guy with the fur hat, low belt, and a cup to throw out later,
Brown suede shoes man with the phony cigarette.

Words lost to overthought
Stares blank to hell
Count my steps
They're normal like
My breathing right?
And this, too?
Is it normal?
The friends and the lifters and the hats and shoes
don't see anything out of the ordinary?
Because we're them too.
The pair with the sad faces
Counting our steps
Tracing the ground
Looking for breaks in the rhythm
In case

J

A small flower blooms
At the other end of the ocean

I found it there
Willed it to grow

Counted the petals
And measured the stem
Will it be taller next year
When I visit again?

For Paul

Take this, Gabrielle,
And let Paul know
That the object enclosed is for him,
From me.

Tell him not to tell my brother,
I will be fine; there was a bandage in the cupboard.
But more gruesome than expected,
I really wasn't aiming for an artery.

This is to let Paul know
What he means to me.
A simple stroke
In exchange for two big lives.

Ah! And would you let Paul know
Our yellow house will be clean upon his return?
And also let Paul know
I'm sorry I got gore on his good knife.

I'm sure he'll be back,
He left without his raincoat.

Has he told you about me?
You are his favorite girl.
Please. This gift must be left wrapped until you see him,
Or you'll make a mess of it!

Antinuous

Another night.
Another night brings
another day.
Another day I'm forced into accepting this body.

I'd feel at home as a statue.
If I were made of stone
I'd stand amongst the great marble warriors
in their foreign dwellings.
My skin would be gleaming and sculpted.
Only to be warmed by things with such intensity as the sun.

There's this situation of the body I'm dealing with.
To say I'm even dealing with it is a bit much.
I'm ignoring it, frankly.
But it seeps into my connections regardless –
which are already hindered by the fact that
I am a marble statue.
Cold and unwavering.

My dear love,
the woman parts of me don't quite connect to the rest.
I'm afraid to say I love you for your girly disposition.
I'm afraid to admit you play a part in my constructed reality.

My dear love,
it's hard to be in my body
keeping the bugs at bay.
But my toes find sand in the sheets of your bed and
I forget my skin when I lay by you because
you make me feel realer than my flesh.

I am your marble statue.
I'm your Antinous
and you shipped my image to every town in the land
so that the people may mourn my loss

after I so tragically fell into the river.
So that I'm remembered and so you don't have to mourn alone.
It's a kind gesture.
But I wish I could have lived before I had to be made inanimate.

Before I go,
I just ask that you let me hold you like you're small.
And you let me rock you to the setting sun.
Because I am faced with another day of me
and it's hard to be her while I'm nothing more
than a man
carved from a chunk
of cold hard stone.

Thought Plot Rock

My sand slippers take me back
To the place I plot

At the edge of the world
Which is really just an ocean
Which is really just a lake called Michigan

Indifferent unchanged waves
Absorb and absolve
Have answered more of my prayers
Than Zeus or G.O.D. God Jesus God

I'm afraid you think my prayers are performance
I'm worried my sadness comes off scripted
Is it wrong if my mind prompts me to cry?

I don't want to be watched
To be heard
I want my footprints to obey the laws of entropy
And my prayers only to be answered
By the God of my imagination

Do I bank on isolation?
There's no merit there
I'd like to fall into the rhythm of those before me
I want to be a part of the relentless shore

But I'm up on my rock
Where I plot my next thought
And I don't want to live anymore

Justice for Empty

Justice for empty
Unfelt widely
Yet passed over
Out of necessity

What comes from empty?
I ask and Squeeze myself dry

There are no grand gestures,
No climaxes here –
See, that's the idea

The thing that takes you nowhere
And demands that you stay

How can nothing be so big,
Feel so strong?

There's nothing to tell about nothing
But it's a lonely thing that wants
A story too
Justice for empty

I Sat

I sat with the bird
Watched it blink
And we stared into the sun

I sat with the dog
Felt its fine hair
And we sang to the moon

I sat with the lizard
Counted its scales
And we stretched out over the earth

I sat with the flower
Picked at its petals
And apologized for the imposition

Those of Us

I'm at work
With a black hole
The size of a pinprick
Tucked away deep
In the center of my heart
It's over

How many are heartbroken today
We restock shelves
Answer calls
Shake hands
With that pinprick hole
Pulling all the while

Hold For X

My heart is too full
So I'll store it in my stomach
And in my soul

And I can't sleep
The debris is poking my sides
The emotional shrapnel

I will keep it safe
In time let it run off me in the shower
Sweat it out alone

Carry on –

Beam

I live on the landscape
And search for the horizon
I sweat in my bed
And boil my blood

Center of the cyclone
Stillness is my mentor
Bugs and grass
My blankets, pillows

But the heat rises
It weighs me down
Fills my veins
Clouds my brain

When will the rain come?

If This is Freedom

Sun beats down on my brow
Sweat has become my second skin
But unspeakable things
I must do for wind

For if I find no movement
If the trees will not sway
I'll have done this all for nothing
Time lost the only gain

Never again may I hold you
No more tears caught by your sleeve
To make such a sacrifice
For a sail-full of breeze

So bring me the blade
I will not say goodbye
The end of your life
Means the death of mine

In Between

Kicking up sand
Waiting for something to start

Made up a story
To pass the time

And so that we may experience
The Beginning and The End
In between ours

Sweet Melancholy

It's hard to shake melancholy
When it rests so sweet in the soul
Thick warm honey
Slowing the beat of my heart
To a tolerable tempo

Top Half / Ripple

The seagulls fed on crawfish
I found a loose pair of claws
And one-half one
The top half.

I poked its head and it moved
I drove off the remaining two gulls
Give the guy a break
Its nature I know
But can I be a source of mercy for the craw?

First, I positioned it to face
The light shale sky
And misty waves of
The big Great Lake
Then, I thought about air
And I kicked him in.

Foul play! Interference with
The way of things!

But what else have we been
Except for idiots who walk upstream
Go against all best interests
Fight against our humanity

Earth's Most Advanced Brain
At the Top of
Our Top Half

Can we wait and watch?
Pass our final hours
Waiting for the last breath
Dozing into the pale shale sky?

I strive to be a watcher
To let it all wash over me
And be there just to be there
But maybe it is in our
Big Brain Nature
To ripple

Make a dent in the fresh snow
Carve lovers' initials into bark
Draw a dick on a desk
Leave a scar
Break a heart
Leave a scar
Kick the top half into the lake
Throw a bottle in the ocean

It will wash away
It will grow or decay
It will mend and heal and die
It will crash and burn, vaporize and explode
with the rest of the planets when the star hits

But I want you to know
I felt you through the ripple you left
What a pleasure to meet you this way